YOU'LL DO ANYTHING FOR HER

A New Relationship Perspective

OTHER BOOKS FROM THE AUTHORS

You'll Do Anything for Him

A NEW RELATIONSHIP PERSPECTIVE

You'll Do ANYTHING for Her

Dr. Maureen E. Hosier & Berta Hosier Conger

PORTLAND • OREGON
INKWATERPRESS.COM

 *Scan this QR Code for more information on this book.*

Copyright © 2017 by Dr. Maureen E. Hosier, Berta Hosier Conger

Edited by Andrew Durkin
Cover and interior design by Masha Shubin
Man Silhouette ® nemetse. BigStockPhoto.com. Heart and Watercolor texture from Pixabay.

All rights reserved. No part of this book may be reproduced or transmitted in any form or by any means whatsoever, including photocopying, recording or by any information storage and retrieval system, without written permission from the publisher and/or author. The views and opinions expressed in this book are those of the author(s) and do not necessarily reflect those of the publisher, and the publisher hereby disclaims any responsibility for them. Neither is the publisher responsible for the content or accuracy of the information provided in this document. Contact Inkwater Press at inkwater.com. 503.968.6777

Publisher: Inkwater Press | www.inkwaterpress.com

Paperback   ISBN-13 978-1-62901-451-7 | ISBN-10 1-62901-451-6
Kindle   ISBN-13 978-1-62901-450-0 | ISBN-10 1-62901-450-8

Printed in the U.S.A.

1 3 5 7 9 10 8 6 4 2

*For all of us who learned to give up ourselves
and to do anything for those we love.*

CONTENTS

A New Relationship Perspective	xv
Chapter 1: The Patterns of Your Relationship	1
The Attraction	1
You'll Do Anything to Be with Her—A One-Person Relationship Perspective	3
The Infatuation Period—In Honeymoon	6
It Doesn't Last	8
The Connection between You Changes—You Feel She's Not Thinking about You	9
The Connection between You Changes—You Feel She Wants Too Much from You	13
The Connection between You Changes—When Something in Your Life Together Changes	15
The Connection between You Changes—When She Changes, You Change and Confront Her	16
Chapter 2: Relationship Perspectives	25
A Two-Person Relationship Perspective	25
The One-Person Relationship Perspective and Cycle: Why You Give Up Your Self	32

Your Emotional Self Is Your Little Kid	44
Understanding You and Your One-Person Relationship: A Recap	48
Chapter 3: You Have a Choice	51
Chapter 4: Something New—Taking Care of Your Self	52
Chapter 5: The Possibility of Something More—A Two-Person Relationship	60
Addendum: A New Relationship Perspective	65
What if You Don't Make It Together	65
A Place to Start—Seeking Professional Help	67
Additional Thoughts to Consider	73
About the Authors	77
Acknowledgments	81
Resources	83
Further Readings	85

If there are physical threats, out-of-control rages, or violence in your relationship, call the National Domestic Violence Hotline for referrals in your local area. They can guide you and your family toward safety. They are available 24/7.

1-800-799-7233
TTY 1-800-787-3224

http://www.thehotline.org

http://www.loveisrespect.org
(for teens and young adults)

If your partner is lying to you, stealing from you, addicted to drugs or alcohol, having a long-term affair or series of affairs, or is verbally or physically abusive, the consequences of these substantial and difficult behaviors must be addressed by you first.

It is your responsibility to protect yourself and your dependents from your partner's inability to care about anyone but herself.

You cannot change her, nor can you wait for her to change.

No matter your circumstances, even if you're not

sure what's happening and just need someone to talk to, we encourage you to consider individual therapy, counseling in your religious affiliation, or a recovery program specific to your needs.

DISCLAIMER

This book is not intended to provide personalized professional psychiatric or psychological counseling, advice, or services. The coauthors specifically disclaim any liability, loss, or risk, personal or otherwise, that is incurred as a consequence, directly or indirectly, of the use and application of any of the contents of this book.

The information and content of this book is intended for informational purposes only and is in the nature of a self-help book rather than a treatment service. If you need therapy or psychiatric consultation, we recommend you contact a licensed mental health professional or religious counselor. The advice of your doctor or therapist or religious affiliation should always be considered when it comes to your health-care and relationship decisions, and information received in the form of a self-help book or similar publication, even when produced by licensed professionals, is not personalized and can in no way be considered treatment for mental health problems or relationship issues. The authors and publishers of this book provide this information and content exclusively for educational, informational, and self-help purposes, and do not represent this book as a treatment service.

The information is general in nature and provided only to give you a starting point for further reading and/or seeking help from a qualified professional in relation to your personal circumstances.

Dearest,

What I want most is to feel cared about and loved by you.

I've tried everything, but it's not working.

What more can I do?

I love you so much, but I don't feel like there are two of us in our relationship.

Me

A NEW RELATIONSHIP PERSPECTIVE

This book sets forth a framework of understanding for people who want to know why they don't feel loved and cared about when they give their partner all their focus, attention, caring, understanding, consideration, and love.

Doing anything for her is your style of relating.

Throughout my professional career, I observed many similarities between my own personal relationship experiences, my sister's relationship experiences, and those of my clients.

It was emotionally painful to listen as my clients of all sexual orientations used words such as "unhealthy," "dysfunctional," or "codependent." Many of them talked about themselves or referred to their partners as "passive-aggressive," "borderline," or "narcissistic."

These words tended to trap those individuals into thinking that there was something wrong with them or their partner.

I then began to describe what was happening in their relationships without labels, and more in terms of growing and changing their perspectives.

My observations and understandings converged into a desire to write a book about what was happening for many of us.

I came to believe that relationships are important opportunities to grow emotionally by learning how to take care of one's self. Growing emotionally requires that I stop trying to get love from the outside, and instead focus on giving love to myself.

When I decided to write a book on relationships, I asked for my sister's help.

As we began to dissect and discuss the experiences and issues of my clients, who were in great emotional pain because their relationships were not working, we began to identify and organize a framework that would best explain what was happening for those who would do anything for their partner.

The starting point was how each person in the couple was raised and how they learned to relate with their parents.

As we began writing, multiple relationship issues came up between us that we, ourselves, had to experience and understand. We had to put words to what was happening for us as individuals and as sisters. And we had to navigate our way through our separate experiences with our parents, and in our own important relationships.

As a result, the layout and narrative of our book reflects the understandings and intimacy of those experiences.

So we are going to talk to you as if we are sitting and talking together. You've come to us because you want to understand why, despite your willingness to do anything for her, your relationship is not working.

You want to know what's happening, why you are in so much emotional pain, and why you're feeling alone.

We will be telling you about you, and how you relate . . . what you may be feeling, thinking, and experiencing, and what you may have experienced growing up to develop these patterns of behaving, thinking, and feeling.

We will also be telling you about how you got stuck, as a child, in your formative emotional development, which now causes you to keep relating in the same way in your important adult relationships.

Our objective is to help you think about your relationship perspective and become aware of your "giving" style, and the patterns of relating that make you willing to do anything for her.

Going forward, we have intentionally split the word "yourself" into two separate words, to help you to focus on *your self*.

It allows us to emphasize and remind you that you have a *self* . . . separate from her.

Highlighting this separation also allows for more effective self-analysis.

You do have needs, feelings, thoughts, preferences, ideas, and concerns that you won't and can't talk to her about.

Our book is a starting point for you to begin to think about you.

For you . . . to remember your childhood experiences, just as we had to do, and then understand how they have been carried forward into how you relate with your partner.

In effect, we have created a shortcut, and provided a possible emotional road map to understanding what might be happening for you with your partner. We have deliberately restated certain sections of our chapters, to help you take in what we are saying.

In addition, our writing style generally consists of one-sentence paragraphs, to encourage you to slow down and pause . . . to think about your feelings and experiences.

We also want to acknowledge that some of our readers are not going to identify with all of the relating behaviors of someone who is willing to do anything for their partner, as we describe them.

But we'll be close enough to your relating dynamics so

that you can begin to think about why you do things her way, and why you're in a relationship with her.

Some of you are not going to agree with all of her relating behaviors as we describe them.

Similarly, some of you may find that you do not relate to our description of how you were raised.

And yet something you experienced at home or at school made you into someone who is not your authentic self in your important relationships.

You desperately need to be in a relationship, and you'll do anything for her, no matter the consequences.

As you read, you may find your self getting stuck on or not connecting with the way we describe things. If this is true, then we suggest you put the book down. Finding disagreement with our words may be your way to avoid and deny the pain you're feeling.

Or maybe you're not a person who thinks of your self as doing anything for your partner.

Or maybe you're not ready to listen and take in what might be happening for you. If that's the case, we understand your hesitation. Begin again when you're ready to feel our words.

Chapter 1 provides descriptions of why you'll do anything for her, and the common experiences and patterns of relating when you focus on her.

Your connection with her begins with the highest of emotional highs: a phase we call "In Honeymoon."

But it doesn't last. And the connection between you changes.

You experience the lowest of emotional lows when you feel she doesn't consider you, and doesn't include you in her life.

Or when she wants too much from you.

Or when something in your life together changes.

Or when she changes, and you confront her about how you're feeling.

Chapter 2 describes how your relationship perspective, with its built-in style and patterns, is passed down from generation to generation, to the children who are raised in a family where one person is in charge.

It also describes a more satisfying relationship perspective.

Chapter 3 reminds you that you have a choice.

Chapter 4 offers you . . . something new.

Chapter 5 offers the possibility of something more for you both.

CHAPTER 1

THE PATTERNS OF YOUR RELATIONSHIP

The Attraction

All you want in life is to be in a loving relationship.

You're happiest when you're with someone.

You need to love.

And you need to feel loved and cared for in return.

You meet a woman.

She pays attention to you.

The idea of who she is and what she can bring to you and your life excites you.

Thrilling thoughts of dating her, being in love, and making a forever commitment enter your mind.

When she focuses on you, you try to contain your excitement and hope, but it's no use. Somehow, you already know that you and she will be great together.

2 | You'll Do Anything for Her

You'll be a good partner for her.

Focusing on her.

Being there for her.

Helping and supporting her.

Taking care of her and meeting her needs.

Accommodating her.

Deferring to her and following her lead.

You'll Do Anything to Be with Her—A One-Person Relationship Perspective

In those first exciting moments with her, you "give up your self."

You deny authentic parts of your self . . . your needs, your feelings, your thoughts, your preferences, your ideas, your voice, and your power.

You give up your self to go along with everything she wants and needs.

You give her the dominant position and make her needs and her feelings more important than yours.

Whatever she needs, you give.

Whatever she wants, you accommodate.

You just want to make it easy for her to be with you. Easy for her to like you and love you.

All to make the relationship work for her.

She becomes your life.

You're thinking about her—and the future you might have together—all the time.

We call this type of relationship perspective a "one-person relationship."

A one-person relationship is either all about her or all about you.

Either you focus on her needs and feelings, or she focuses on your needs and feelings.

Without hesitation, you focus on her needs and feelings and agree to a one-person relationship, with her in charge, leading the way.

This is how you love. This is how you relate.

This is your way of trying to ensure she's happy with you.

This is your way of trying to take care of her.

It's how you try to avoid conflict with her.

It's how you try to avoid hurting her feelings.

Men and women who give up themselves can be attracted to others like themselves, but quite often, they tend to be attracted to women who are self-assured, who know what they want, and who are in charge.

Women who are comfortable showing their irritation, frustration, and anger if you make a suggestion, say what you want, or express your opinion.

We will explain why you're attracted to this relationship dynamic later.

You may not have given much thought to who or how you are in your relationship. You may not even acknowledge that you give up your self, because what you do feels so natural.

You may, however, have thought about your self as being an accommodator, people-pleaser, or enabler. You may know your self to be codependent.

You might even worry that you're a doormat.

We encourage you to set these labels aside and learn something new about your self and your relationship perspective by thinking about how you were raised.

We want to help you explore what's happening inside of you: why you're willing to subordinate your self and put your self aside so easily, to make the relationship "work."

We want you to understand there is no judgment or blame about how you relate or how she relates.

Giving up your self for her, and for your family and friends, is your style of relating. It is the relationship perspective that you had to take on as a child, as you learned to be in a relationship with your parents.

Similarly, your partner's style of relating with you is to be in charge. She too learned this style of relating with her parents.

There is nothing "bad" or "good" about either of these relating styles. They simply reflect the relating dynamics and emotional development that a child learns in the millions of interactions with their parents.

The Infatuation Period—In Honeymoon

Her attraction to you and your attraction to her is magnetic.

The passion. The touching. The sensuality. The affection.

Looking into each other's eyes is a dream come true.

You love the emotional and physical connection you have with her. You feel so cared for and considered and accepted.

She wants to be with you—and you want to be with her—all the time.

She focuses on your well-being.

She's generous and giving.

She talks with you, about you.

She includes you.

She wants to know what you'd like to do.

She wants to know what your thoughts are.

You feel so alive when her focus and attention is on you.

You feel loved.

You feel special.

You feel accepted and safe, maybe for the first time.

You trust her, and you open up emotionally.

You feel so in love, and you're happy that you're getting the intimacy and closeness that you've yearned for.

Here is the laughter, playfulness, and companionship you've always wanted.

Her strong and confident presence brings life to your life. You spend all your time together, learning about and doing things you never would have done on your own.

With her, you know the two of you can make anything happen.

Everything is perfect, and you don't feel like you're giving up anything, especially not your self.

In those precious In Honeymoon moments, you have the loving "us" connection you've always wanted.

You're feeling loved, like you've never felt before.

All is wonderful In Honeymoon.

It Doesn't Last

In Honeymoon ends.

There are many different reasons why.

From your perspective, the loving "us" connection between you changes.

You feel cut off and alone.

We will explore what you feel in several one-person relationship patterns that occur when In Honeymoon ends.

The Connection between You Changes— You Feel She's Not Thinking about You

She does what she wants, and you're not included.

She's focused on her work, her friends, and her interests, and she spends more and more time away from you.

It feels like she's not as emotionally connected with you.

You feel like she's not as caring and affectionate.

When she's with you, she talks about what's happening in her life; she tells you what she's going to do and how things are going to be.

She says she loves you, and you know you love her, too, but you're in a different place now.

You miss her.

You don't feel cared about.

You don't feel loved.

It feels like she's taking you for granted.

Inside, you feel rejected, insecure, little-kid scared, and utterly alone.

Maybe even angry, because what she's focused on feels more important to her than you are.

You work hard to not get emotional when you're feeling forgotten and not included.

Instead, you keep your emotions hidden and under control. And you do your best to understand and accept her wanting to be away from you.

You try to comfort your self with the thought that In Honeymoon never lasts.

So you don't say anything. You don't want to ruin the moments you can have with her when she comes back.

But you really want to tell her, she's changed.

And you really want to tell her how hard it is when she doesn't want to be with you . . . when she tells you what's going to happen in the relationship.

You just can't understand why she's not thinking about you, why she's not missing you—especially when you felt her so focused on you, so connected with you during In Honeymoon.

Now it's like you don't exist for her.

But you love her.

Believing this is what she needs, you convince your self you want it for her, too.

So you extend your self even more to accept the "new" her.

You try hard to love her unconditionally.

You try to stop thinking about what you're feeling—your doubts and concerns.

And you try to recommit to accommodating her every need, and following her lead.

And you continue to believe that doing anything and everything for her will help her know and feel how much you're there for her, how much you consider her, and how much you love her.

You hope that she will feel how much you take care of her, and that she will finally realize how much she needs you.

You hope she will want to reconnect with you and spend more time with you.

You keep going for months, and maybe even years, and support her in what she needs to be happy.

Even though you both know that things aren't right between you, there's no talking about much of anything—except what's going on for her, and what she needs and wants.

You want, more than anything, to feel loved and cared about again.

But you don't know how to get there.

You're unable to have a real conversation with her.

You're unable to leave her.

You're alone . . . with someone you love.

You're in deep pain, yearning to feel loved, and not understanding why this is happening.

You know you need just a little bit of her time, focus, and attention to make things alright.

You always hope In Honeymoon will come back. But it doesn't.

And in this time of emotional and physical disconnection, maybe one or both of you looks to another person—someone who listens to your problems and understands your loneliness.

Affairs are very common in one-person relationships.

The Connection between You Changes— You Feel She Wants Too Much from You

She dominates your life.

She dominates your every moment.

You become her only focus.

She wants all of your time.

She needs you for everything.

She wants what she wants.

To make the relationship work, you go along with what she wants.

But now, things don't ever seem to go exactly as she wants them to.

Nothing you say or do is ever right for her.

She blames you.

What she told you she wanted, she denies ever having said.

When she asks what you'd like to do, she either ignores what you say or criticizes you for having made such a stupid suggestion.

As hard as you try to do everything for her, and give her all you've got, it's just never enough.

It's just never good enough to get her to love and care about you in return.

She keeps wanting more.

And when you make any attempt to create some emotional or physical space between you, she falls apart or gets angry.

You're caught in your own mixed feelings. It's an emotional battle.

You still love her, but you're drowning in her demands and restrictions, and you feel like you're going crazy.

You obsess about what's happening: is it you or her?

Then you wonder whether you should try to take care of your self and leave—but choosing your self, in that way, makes you feel so guilty and selfish that you won't even consider it.

The Connection between You Changes—When Something in Your Life Together Changes

She changes when some outside influence or stressor breaks into your In Honeymoon paradise.

It could be a single event, or a combination of events. It could be money problems, career demands, a job termination, a new baby, or medical problems.

She moves away from you at a time when you need to be talking more and working things out together.

She shuts down and can't or won't talk about what's happening.

Maybe you can't talk about it either, knowing she'll get upset with you if you try.

Maybe you don't know what to say because you don't want to hurt her feelings.

You know you can't leave her because you feel she needs you so desperately.

You keep going, for her sake, and you do your best to power through the hard times on your own.

You keep things as normal as possible, and make sure her every need in your day-to-day life together gets met. You wait and hope for months, and even years, for her to emotionally and physically come back to you.

The Connection between You Changes—When She Changes, You Change and Confront Her

You're hurt and unhappy, and have been for a while.

You know you've been more than generous.

You've been taking care of her and trying to make things easier for her.

You've been giving her all your focus and attention when she needs it.

You've been giving her the space and distance she needs when she needs that, too.

You've done everything you know how to do for her.

But it just doesn't feel like there are two of you in the relationship.

You feel like you're alone and on your own.

You still desperately want to feel that loving "us" connection with her again.

So you decide that you have to talk to her. You have to make her understand!

Maybe you're little-kid angry, just wanting to blast her because you've held on too long and are feeling resentful.

Maybe you're little-kid scared because you're ready to say something, but you don't want to hurt her feelings or make her mad.

You know it's not going to go well.

You know she's going to be upset with anything you say.

So you try to find the perfect thing to say at the perfect moment, in the hope that she might listen.

Some of you don't try so hard. You just explode!

But no matter what you do, she gets angry.

And you both—get *in it!*

She says she doesn't understand why you're saying anything at all and why it's such a big deal for you. She is shocked that there's anything wrong.

And she's adamant that she did nothing wrong. Then you're adamant that you didn't say she did anything wrong.

Then you try again to tell her how you feel.

You raise your voice—maybe whining or begging her to listen.

You're determined to be heard.

You're determined to make her listen!

You try to explain that you are hurt by her being

away so much and making decisions about your future without including you.

But she will not give up any part of herself to listen.

Then things you did and things she did come up, and there's a barrage of accusations about each other's inadequacies in loving and caring.

Both of you demand what you want, like little kids.

Out-of-control little kids.

You bicker, argue, and yell. Maybe you swear. Maybe you call each other names.

You challenge her. You want to exist too!

In it! happens again and again because you have found your voice.

Your persistence in trying to talk to her, be heard, and get her to understand your side of things freezes the relationship in a constant battle.

In it! invades every facet of your life.

As your little-kid emotions get called to the surface more and more, you're *in it!* before you know it.

And the craziness between you can start over anything, at any time.

You're having a good time together and then her anger comes out of nowhere and destroys your good feelings—over something you know you didn't do or intend, but she thinks you did.

Or you get mad over something she did, ruining her good feelings.

And *in it!* starts all over again.

The reality of getting *in it!* is that neither one of you will be controlled, talked over, cut off, or prevented from saying what you need to say.

Neither one of you will tolerate any tone of frustration or anger. Neither one of you is willing to be ignored, blamed, or accused of not being a good enough partner.

And neither one of you can tolerate the other being a know-it-all and never wrong. And neither one of you will take responsibility for your out-of-control behaviors.

Getting *in it!* over and over again never leads to getting heard and understood.

. . . And getting *in it!* doesn't have to be about yelling at each other.

When you ask her for what you want, or tell her how you're feeling, she's got nothing to say.

She ignores you. Silently, she projects her anger, making sure you leave her alone, because you know she's never going to talk about it. She's never going to listen.

Her cutting you off triggers your own silent blast of *in it!* You silently rage at her stubbornness and inability to talk to you about something so important—your thoughts and your feelings.

You desperately want to have a part in the relationship, too.

Her silence leaves you with nothing to hold on to and nowhere to go.

You've been rejected. Again.

You're still alone.

And still trying to recover and figure things out on your own.

In it!, whether angry or silent, lands you in a very familiar place.

You're stuck in your head, replaying what you should have done differently. Whether it's for hours or days, you can't stop criticizing your self, judging your self, and wondering whether you were right to say something in the first place.

You worry, and then worry some more . . . about whether you're being selfish.

Then you criticize your self because you didn't say what you really wanted to say.

And what can you do to stop shouting at her? It just comes rushing out of you.

Then you think you should apologize for getting so emotional, and for hurting her feelings and making her angry.

So you think about how you can make things better.

But then you get confused and begin to have doubts about trying to change things for your self, because what she said begins to make much more sense than what you tried to say.

Then you begin to remember the words you said, which she twisted around and used against you to blame you and make everything your fault.

You spin in circles, thinking about you, thinking about her, and thinking about the relationship. You get more and more confused and overwhelmed and think everything is your fault.

Then you come back to the same decision you've made over and over again, knowing it's just easier, if you do things her way.

In the aftermath of each *in it!* battle, you know you have to give up your self again and wait, and wait, and wait, until she decides to talk to you. When she does, it's about something trivial and unimportant.

That's your clue that everything is temporarily okay. You feel comfortable enough to say something trivial and unimportant too—to let her know you've calmed down as well.

But you also know, it's not okay for you to say anything about what happened.

In it! is about you finally trying to make your self known to her.

You need to exist in the relationship.

You need her to understand your side of things.

You need her to know that you had a different experience than she did. And that it all makes sense.

Now you'll do anything and everything to make that happen *for your self.*

You're willing to stand up for your self.

You push your self, and what you feel, on her.

But she still won't listen to you.

The worst feeling is knowing she *likes* you taking care of her, being there for her, and waiting for her. But you're exhausted from giving her all your focus and attention.

And you're tired of getting nothing back.

Why isn't she there for you? Why doesn't she even think about you in the way you need her to?

Somehow you have to get her to understand.

As the *in it!* moments accumulate, nothing in the way

of repairing or rebuilding your relationship can get accomplished.

At times, it feels like you hate the essence of each other.

Every bitter and unresolved interaction fuels the next outburst, and then you end up back in the same lonely place, again.

After many debilitating confrontations, loud or silent, one of you can't stand it anymore and decides to leave for good.

You separate.

Then . . .

Maybe you get back together.

Then you both are back *in it!*

And maybe you break up again.

And go back to one another again . . . and again . . . and again.

In it! is an emotional clash.

It is the direct consequence of you trying to exist for your self.

It is the direct consequence of you demanding that she change, demanding that she listen and understand your experience and your side of things, and demanding that she include you in the relationship and spend more time with you.

For you, getting *in it!* is progress . . . a beginning.

You're beginning to discover your self, and value what you want and need. You're beginning to want to exist . . . for you.

But you're stuck repeating the same hopeless pattern over and over again.

In it! is just another pattern, another sign that your one-person relationship is not working . . . for you.

CHAPTER 2

RELATIONSHIP PERSPECTIVES

A Two-Person Relationship Perspective

Before we talk about how you were raised and the origins of your one-person relationship, we will describe the beginnings of a more satisfying experience: a two-person relationship.

This chapter is written as if you are the child in this two-person relationship; it may be emotionally difficult to read.

There was a time—when you were a baby and then a little kid—when everyone else was bigger than you.

It was a time when you needed to be the center of your parents' world, and everything was about you.

Your parent or parents focused on you.

They were dependable and reliable—they were there for you when you needed them.

They wanted to be there for you, so you felt safe, secure, and loved.

You felt a constancy, an accumulation of good feelings and positive experiences in your parents' affection, love, interaction, and enjoyment of you. You were validated by their willingness to spend lots of time with you—taking care of you, holding you, looking into your eyes, talking to you, reading to you, laughing with you, and playing with you.

Even when they couldn't immediately meet your needs for physical comfort, social interaction, emotional holding, and understanding, they felt your emotional distress and came to you as soon as they could. They used hugs, soothing words, and apologies to repair any disconnection with you. They comforted you and understood why you felt the way you felt.

Even though you may not have had any words for it yet, you *felt* their caring.

You *felt* them wanting to be there for you.

Along with their ongoing focus and attention and support, you experienced their reasonable boundaries and limits, matched to your developmental needs, emotional maturity, and age.

As you got older and learned how to talk, they helped you understand that using words set you free to be your self and explore your world.

You were encouraged to express what you needed and wanted, what made you happy, and what hurt you and made you feel bad.

They listened because they wanted you to be you.

They listened because they didn't want to change you.

Your parents taught you that your feelings and emotional reactions had meaning. When you were ready, they helped you put words to what you were feeling.

They wanted to help you understand why you felt the way you felt. They wanted to help you learn to calm your self, so you could say what you needed.

You learned that being able to talk with them made you feel important. Talking with them helped you to trust what you were thinking and feeling, and it helped you make better decisions.

Their listening to you made you feel good about your self. And kept you from feeling alone and on your own.

No was a very important word for you both. Whether you said *no* or they said *no*, you talked about your differences. You talked about what you were thinking and why you felt that way. And they talked about what they were thinking and why they felt that way.

Even when your parents had the last word, you still felt they cared for you, though it may have taken a while to sort through your feelings to figure that out.

Over time, you learned to trust and consider your parents' thoughts and feelings.

Those positive experiences and feelings of being heard, understood, loved, accepted, and valued provided the foundation for your growing sense of *your self*.

A sense of you.

A confident you.

Embraced by your parents' nurturing, you grew stronger emotionally.

When you felt disconnected from them, they recognized that uncomfortable space between you and talked about it when you were ready. You both learned what had happened and why, and you worked together to understand how to handle similar situations differently in the future.

When your parents happened to be emotionally reactive to something you had done or not done, they apologized and took responsibility for their over-the-top reactions. And they tried to not handle things that way again.

You too learned to take responsibility for your actions and reactions that were inappropriate and maybe hurtful to them.

You learned to apologize. And you tried to handle things differently the next time, too.

With time, you came to value your own needs and feelings. And you learned to recognize and value the needs and feelings of your parents and others.

In all these ways, you got enough of your emotional needs met and validated to feel that you were loved, lovable, appreciated, and valued.

Your parents then slowly stepped back. They trusted you to make your own decisions. At the same time, they were there to help and support you in any way you needed.

You gained a growing sense of confidence in taking care of your self and being out in the world on your own. This was possible because you were given the understanding and support to make your own "mistakes" and learn from them.

You learned that you could always go to them to talk about any confusion or misunderstanding.

There was no blame or judgment—just encouraging support to help you understand your course of action.

You came to understand that you and your parents could exist separately in the same moment: *you* and *them*.

They, with their own needs, feelings, thoughts, preferences, ideas, voices, and power.

You, with your own needs, feelings, thoughts, preferences, ideas, voice, and power.

With time and years of positive experiences, a caring and close connection was formed, deeply rooted in your parents' wanting to be there for you.

You felt a loving "us" connection with them.

This warm and close connection was your *first* and most important place of learning.

This was a safe place to be you and learn about you.
It was a safe place to learn about your needs, feelings, thoughts, ideas, voice, and power.

You were always learning.

You were always growing stronger emotionally.

It was a safe place to develop your self-esteem and self-confidence.

A safe place to learn to take care of your self.

A safe place to be you.

A safe place to leave when you were ready.

You were born with the potential to be your self.
And because you were able to have a voice with your parents, you learned how to be *for* your self, and how to feel a part of every experience with them *as* your self.

Your strong and loving "us" connection with
your parents, you and them, was built upon your experiences and feelings of being accepted, considered, loved, valued, and understood in a "two-person relationship."

Your experiences of a strong and loving "us" connection are inside of you.

You don't feel alone or on your own.

You are there for your self, and your parents are there for you, too.

The two-person relationship perspective that you experienced with your parents, you bring with you into all your relationships.

The One-Person Relationship Perspective and Cycle: Why You Give Up Your Self

This chapter may also be difficult to read, because you experienced a one-person relationship.

As a child, you learned a specific way of relating that required you to focus outside your self. You learned to focus solely on the needs and feelings of someone else.

Keep in mind that your growing-up experiences are unique to you and may not be as difficult as we describe in this chapter. Unfortunately, your experiences may have been much worse.

You grew up in a one-person household, where your mom, dad, brother, sister, other family member, or even someone not related to you was in charge.

That dominant person had demands and expectations of you and became your "important parent." They got upset or hurt you when you didn't do what you were told.

They may have judged you and told you that you were bad, wrong, dumb, and stupid. Or maybe they criticized you, picked on you, laughed at you, teased you, or embarrassed you in front of others.

If you were a latchkey kid, your important parent still found a way to make crystal clear what you were to do and how you were to be.

Through their actions and words, your important

parent taught you there was only one way to relate: do things his or her way.

They were in charge.

You were a little kid.

You were not allowed to exist as your self with them.

You had to give up your self to focus on them, meet their demands, and do what they wanted.

You had to obey.

You experienced a one-person relationship with your important parent.

You had to learn fast.

Questions were not allowed. No explanations were given.

You automatically said *yes* because you were afraid to say *no*.

You were afraid your important parent might turn away from you and ignore you. You were afraid they might reject you or abandon you.

Or you were afraid they might hurt you, if you didn't do what they wanted.

There was no connection or closeness with your important parent.

There was no talking. There were no kind words, and no comforting touches or affection.

There was no caring about your emotional needs or feelings. When you were hurt and upset by them, they didn't comfort you.

When you made mistakes, they got mad. They said it was your fault: "You should have known better."

When things didn't go right, they blamed you. Their anger, their words, and their tone made you feel dumb and stupid.

If you somehow happened to make the mistake of choosing your self, you were told that you were selfish and should be ashamed.

You learned it was mandatory to not ask for anything and to not need anything.

And no matter what you did, it was never good enough.

It was always your fault.

You learned you were alone.

There was no one to talk to . . . about anything.

You felt like you didn't belong.

You never really felt safe.

You were always anxious, off-balance, and unsure of your self. You always felt inadequate.

You felt like a nobody with someone you loved.

You spent lots of time in your head—thinking, worrying, replaying what you did to make them so angry. You tried to figure out what you did that wasn't right. You tried to figure out what you should have done.

You tried to make sense of things.

So you blamed your self, over and over again, for not remembering the "right" thing to do or say. For being so dumb and stupid. For not being good enough.

And on top of all that, you had to pretend that their words and actions didn't get to you. You didn't want them to know anything about what you were thinking or feeling.

You didn't want them to know anything about the conflicting feelings you had—the sense that something wasn't right.

They told you they knew what was best for you. They were your parents.

So you learned that not saying anything and keeping your emotional reactions hidden was a way to survive.

You learned that being extra helpful and polite and getting good grades helped you stay invisible.

You learned to never share anything about your self with anyone, because it could get back to your parents.

And as you got smarter about how to be with them,

maybe you began to go behind their backs to do things you knew they didn't want you to do. But when you did what you wanted to do, you felt guilty and ashamed. And you worried that they would find out.

Every day you hoped that things would somehow change. You started living ahead of your self, in your head, and fantasizing about how wonderful things would be when your parent or parents magically changed and wanted to be with you and talk to you and care about you.

Or you fantasized about how good your life would be when you left them.

Or maybe you hoped that when you got older, you'd meet someone who would finally make you feel special.

And maybe you felt so hopeless that you wished they were dead. Then you felt guilty about having such horrible thoughts.

Through it all, the only thing you could do to protect your self was to learn to deny your own needs. You learned to shut down your feelings of being hurt, isolated, unseen, unknown, unloved, not valued, and not cared for in the way you needed by your important parent.

All the while, those experiences and feelings were still there, quietly reminding you that you were the problem. You believed that there was something wrong with you, because what you did for them was never enough. It was just never good enough.

But you kept going, trying to do everything they wanted you to do.

You were desperate for any connection with them.

You hoped that if you just kept to your self and didn't say anything, your important parent would see how hard you tried, and acknowledge you for being the good kid you were.

You hoped they would acknowledge the good stuff you did.

But that never happened.

You may have watched a sibling or other parent have the emotional tenacity to stand up for his or her self. You may have seen them arguing, fighting back, trying to hang on to some sense of their self.

But you saw that these things didn't work.

Besides, you didn't ever want to be mean and hurt anyone's feelings, like yours had been hurt.

You especially did not want to hurt your important parent's feelings. There would be hell to pay for that.

So you silently vowed to never get *in it!* if you could help it.

If you couldn't help it and did stand up for your self, you did it because you just needed your important parent to listen and understand your perspective. You needed him or her to consider you, to know that you weren't wrong, that you weren't bad, that what you said or did made sense.

Eventually, though, you probably had to cave in and give up your self again, because getting *in it!* was hopeless. Nothing ever changed.

As you got older, you may have found ways to stay after school or hang out with your friends so you wouldn't have to go home. Or you just held on for as long as you could and then escaped and left home.

Maybe you got married and then found your self in another one-person relationship.

In any case, your important parent controlled and managed your life.

You were the child.

They were bigger than you.

They were in charge of your one-person relationship.

The relationship was all about them and not at all about you.

They existed, so you couldn't.

Their rules and their demands became your way of life—the very structure of your life. That was who you were to be. That was how you were to be and what you were to be.

You did your best to meet your important parent's

demands and expectations and follow their lead, because you were emotionally and physically dependent on them for your survival. You desperately wanted that person to be happy with you.

At the very least, you wanted them not to be mad at you. So of course, you did what your important parent wanted, and what was right for them.

This is how you've come to deny your self.

This is how you don't allow your self to have a voice, feelings, or needs—or even to value what you're thinking or feeling.

This is how you've come to not exist for your self.

This is how you've come to not exist with others.

What you experienced growing up in your one-person relationship was ingrained in you. Giving up your self and hiding your feelings has become your automatic and protective way of being.

What you experienced with your important parent you bring with you into all your relationships.

The only thing you're certain of is that you desperately need someone in your life.

And you still need to feel accepted, loved, and cared about.

It's important that you understand that your mother or father (or both) most likely experienced a one-person relationship with one or both of their parents—and so on back through your family history.

They too had to give up themselves and not exist when they were little kids, because that's the way it was for them.

As children, your parents learned that they didn't have to give up themselves to their own children.

They also learned that only one person could be in charge in their adult relationships.

So you may have watched one of your parents give up his or her self and not say anything to defend you or themselves.

But there may have been an exception for you. You may have felt loved because your important parent favored you, while dominating your brothers, sisters, and other parent. Nevertheless, you learned to be afraid of your important parent and made every effort to not upset them.

Maybe you have "forgotten" how awful it was to be controlled by your important parent, so you don't think about that part of your life. You only remember and talk about the good times.

Maybe there were no good times.

Here's yet another scenario. You may have felt guilty about how hard your parents worked to give you a life better than the one they had. So you felt the need to put your self aside and do the things they needed you to do. You felt you had no choice but to become the person they wanted you to be.

You couldn't disappoint them.

And you still feel the pressure to be the person they wanted you to be.

We want to stress here that growing up in a one-person household is not about your parents being blamed or judged. It is not about your parents being right or wrong, good or bad.

It's only about you having missed out on a vital part of your emotional development. It's not what your parents ever intended, because they, too, missed out on a vital part of their emotional development.

They didn't even know it was possible to relate in a different way.

A two-person relationship was not in their experience.

Your parents learned from their parents that it was their responsibility to make sure that you were "tough enough" to make it through life, just as they had to do.

Your parents believed they had to make you emotionally strong, because they were taught that showing any emotions made you weak.

They raised you in the only way they knew how.

They also raised you knowing that their success in all their endeavors was dependent upon whether they were perceived as good parents with well-behaved children. Image was critical to your important parent.

And just as they had experienced, you weren't allowed to have needs or feelings, or to connect with your authentic self. Nor did you get the opportunity to feel loved, and in their love, have a sense of your self.

You didn't learn who you were because your important parent's demands and expectations prevented you from experiencing your inner emotional world and your outer physical world with confidence and feelings of worth.

You didn't get those necessary opportunities to say out loud what you wanted, or what was right for you, or what worked for you.

In fact, you may still hear your parents' harsh words. This is how you manage your own behavior—how you keep your self in line. You're always trying to do what you think you should do—always looking for the rules in your head, always trying to figure out the "right" thing to do.

You came to understand that giving up your self and not existing was your only way to try to connect with them. Giving up your self was an act of love.

Now, as an adult, you're still giving up your self as a way to give love and finally get love. You're looking over and over again for that loving "us" connection that you didn't get, or that you didn't get enough of.

You're waiting and hoping for someone, like your

important parent, to love you. To acknowledge you. To listen to you. To value you. To accept you.

To *want* to know you.

So you can feel safe and finally learn to be your self. Out loud.

Whatever your growing-up experiences were, you learned to be the kid your important parent needed you to be.

You changed your self for that person.

You had to. You were raised in a one-person relationship.

It's just how it was.

It was the continuation of a multigenerational cycle of one-person relationships. And it was the beginning of yours.

Your Emotional Self Is Your Little Kid

You got through those many painful experiences with your important parent by shutting down your natural and honest needs, feelings, and emotional reactions.

You had to stuff it all . . . your needs. Your feelings. Your emotions. Your self.

Unconsciously, that created a reservoir of unexpressed pain, needs, feelings, beliefs, disappointments, resentments, fears, anxieties, deep sadness, and anger—maybe even hatred and rage.

This reservoir of feelings and emotions is still present, buried inside you, ready to "go off" with the right trigger.

This emotionally charged place is incredibly sensitive, and vulnerable to you feeling blamed, criticized, yelled at, frightened, put down, dismissed, not recognized, forgotten, and not included.

It's also vulnerable to you feeling rejected, abandoned, and not loved. Not valued or appreciated.

This is the place inside of you that learned to focus on your important parent—to try to take care of them, to not upset them or bother them, and to give them what they wanted.

This is the place that kept you trying to be good enough for your important parent—over and over again.

As an adult, emotionally, you are still that *little kid*.

This little-kid place defines you, most of the time—especially in an important relationship.

So your little-kid place works hard to anticipate and avoid situations where those feelings of being rejected, abandoned, and not loved could come up.

This is the place that holds your deepest yearnings to be heard, understood, and accepted by her.

Now, this is the place that doesn't understand why she doesn't value, accept, and love you the way she did during In Honeymoon.

This is the place that hurts and aches when you feel she's not connected to you.

This is the place that constantly reminds you that you feel inadequate around her and around others.

Now, this is the same place that keeps you trying to get it "right" with her, that keeps you trying to make the relationship work for her, so she would emotionally come back to you.

And as hard as you have tried to *make* her feel your giving and your love, this is the place where you can become reactive and quick to defend your self, or fight back or shut down when you get *in it!*

Over the longer term, this is where you can come to feel depressed and hopeless, anxious and insecure, or isolated and cut off. It is the place of low self-esteem and low self-confidence.

Her anger or her silence, her demands and her expectations, make you feel like a frightened little kid all over again.

Somehow, you knew when you met her, you weren't supposed to be your real self. Even though you felt so loved by her.

You somehow knew if you tried to be your self, you'd challenge her, and then she'd leave you. So you kept to your self and didn't voice your thoughts, feelings, wants, or needs.

And each time you felt unloved and not considered, you worked hard to extend your self and give even more. And with each new experience with her, you learned how to adjust, how to shift, and what words to say to keep things the way she wanted them to be, so she wouldn't reject you or get angry the next time.

And when you had no more left to give, you got *in it!* with her.

Or you stayed and gave up your self and stopped fighting something that would never change.

Or you convinced your self to leave and you did.

When you're ready to change, this is the place where you can come to finally know that you need and want to exist in the relationship too.

But neither one of you can stay out of the repetition of the one-person relationship cycle and patterns, because you both, without awareness, chose someone who would bring those painful past experiences into your present.

This repetition and your feelings of being unloved and not cared about are desperately trying to tell you that giving up your self to make your relationship work for her, is not working for you.

Understanding You and Your One-Person Relationship: A Recap

You've endured feeling alone, afraid, insecure, forgotten, and unloved too many times by your important parent.

These experiences forced you into becoming someone different from who you really are.

You hoped that being older would change everything.

But being an adult didn't change a thing, because you bring into your current relationship your automatic giving-up behaviors conditioned by your one-person relationship experiences with your important parent.

So your little kid always needs to be in someone else's life. You've always been emotionally vulnerable, and guided by what someone else wants and needs—or guided by what you think someone else wants and needs.

In those first exciting moments, when you looked into her eyes and you clicked, you both wanted to be in a relationship. Yes, you will be together, but you're not going to be in the relationship that you'd hoped for. For you, that click, that attraction, that happiness is the recognition that you have found someone you know how to be with.

Without realizing it, you fit with her because she's your new important parent, and you're still your little kid.

Your little kid looked toward your new relationship

as the most important thing—the thing you needed to make it through life. Your little kid hoped for emotional safety, and finally, an emotional connection to someone who showed you their love—love that you could feel.

Your one-person relationship is, and has been, all about you and what you hoped to get from her.

During In Honeymoon, you felt loved. You felt important, accepted, considered, and cared for. You felt known. You felt included. You felt special, and that you belonged.

You did not know that underneath all those good feelings, you were not your authentic self.

When she paid attention to you, you automatically took up your assigned role based on your early relating experiences. And just as it was during your early relating experiences with your important parent, she was in charge.

As an adult, you still give up your self and allow your self to be controlled.

You allow her to be in charge.

You allow her to lead the way.

When In Honeymoon ends and you feel the change in your loving "us" connection, you drown in your aloneness and guilt.

You believe it's all your fault.

And without a sense of your self in the relationship, you feel lost and alone.

Your yearning to feel loved, and your little-kid hope that things will work out—your denial system—have been covering up what's happening to you in the present.

When you finally begin to connect with your emotional pain and the experiences from your past, you will realize it's happening again with her.

You're caught in a one-person relationship trap, giving up more and more of your self to be with someone you love.

As a little kid you had to try to ignore or cut off that pain, because you had no choice.

As an adult, you're still thinking and reacting from your little-kid place, trying to ignore the emotional pain.

You haven't yet realized that as an adult, you are allowed to relate differently in your relationships.

You're allowed to exist in your relationships—to be your self and take care of you.

As an adult, you're responsible for how you feel.

You're the only one who can do anything about your emotional pain.

She is not the person who needs to change . . . you are.

CHAPTER 3

YOU HAVE A CHOICE

Maybe now, you've come to realize that doing anything for her can't and won't ever get you what you want, or change how you feel.

As an adult with your little-kid emotions, you've not been your authentic self—the one who brings your needs, your feelings, your thoughts, your preferences, your ideas, your voice, and your power into your relationship, and who chooses what you want for your self.

If you choose being your self, then your only starting point is to recognize and accept that you are the foundation of your one-person relationship. You have willingly given up your self.

You will have to accept that *not* existing for your self is . . . what's been preventing you from having a two-person relationship.

Only you can change how you feel in your relationship.

It's the only thing you haven't tried to do.

CHAPTER 4

SOMETHING NEW—TAKING CARE OF YOUR SELF

When you choose your self, you have made a decision to turn your focus from the outside to the inside and to be in charge of the quality of your life.

It's been a slow, excruciating, emotionally painful process to finally realize that your little kid can't ever get what you need from her.

That's a profound realization.

People are separate and different from you.

No one has to change for you.

Nor can you change her.

Realizing that you cannot get your needs met from outside of your self begins the process of your moving into unfamiliar emotional territory with your self and with her: learning how to be your authentic self and taking care of your own needs.

Now you can think about you.

Taking care of your self simply means learning about your self in the same way you learned about her.

It means watching and observing your self, but now shifting and adjusting to what feels right for you.

Taking care of your own needs requires that you change . . . again.

Only this time, it will not hurt you to become your self.

You can be interesting to you.

All your learning will take place inside of you.

You will learn to focus your attention first and foremost on you.

You will have to connect your thinking with your feelings.

This will require you to go inside your self and learn what you want. And learn how to ask for what you want.

You will be presenting your truth, your thinking, and your feelings. You will be working through your fear of being alone, and trying not to push her away, because the relationship is still important to you.

You will be always mindful that you don't want to put your self back into the position of having no choice but to give up your self.

And you will be mindful that her caring for you may be different than what you want and need.

When you are thinking about and considering your self, you won't feel alone.

You are with you.

You are inside your self.

You are accommodating you.

You are learning what feels right for you . . . what feels comfortable for you.

You are allowing your self to take your own path.

Remembering that each decision you make is reasonable because you are still learning about what you want.

You'll also learn that your quick responses are your little-kid responses.

By slowing down the reaction time inside your self, which requires practice and patience, you can begin to ask your self, *What do I really want to do for my self?*—as opposed to just saying yes.

If you realize that you have a need to make her happy, did it come out of your little-kid place?

And if you feel you missed a chance to be your self, you can always go back and say "I have second thoughts."

You have to *want* to be there with her as your self. Your authentic self. The person your important parent demanded that you reject and hide.

By connecting your thoughts and feelings, you can begin to live in the present moment.

And begin to build your foundation of understanding . . . your sense of who you are.

This is where self-confidence is explored, nurtured, and created . . . by you.

Because you have come to know who you are, and you trust what you feel.

By living in the moment, you'll begin to observe and understand that anything you do for her will *not* change who she is or what she does. It's always been that way.

You will also learn to eliminate your inner critic, who's been dictating that you should always be focusing on and doing the "right thing" for her—for everybody. And accept that how you were raised makes you want to automatically do the "right thing" for someone else.

You have a choice: do the "right thing" for her or do the "right thing" for you?

With her, you feel alone and on your own. And you've done a darn good job of denying that pain until now.

Is it time to learn how stop all that pain and worrying and doing for someone else?

You will learn that your little-kid feelings and reactions and memories are your warning signals that someone is "expecting" that you do something you may not want to do.

You will learn that the word "no" can be an important word for you when you look inside and see that what was demanded or requested or supposed to be the way they wanted it to be, really doesn't work for you.

"No" becomes a word that defines who you are and what you want for your self, because you have thought about what you want, and your feelings are in agreement with what you want.

You will learn the importance of saying this: "I'm sorry—I can't, but maybe this might work instead."

Or this: "Let me give it some thought and I'll come back with some suggestions."

Or this: "I'd love to help, but I just can't. I'm sorry."

You will learn how to evaluate all the variables that are important in your decision-making. And your decision-making will generally be a slow process of coming to be clear about what you want and need.

You will learn how to take a deep breath and interrupt your little-kid emotions and subsequent reactions by remembering that you don't want to be your little kid.

Then you can get back to thinking about why and what you are doing, and realizing that your past and present have just collided.

Now, in this moment, you want to handle your self differently.

With practice and patience and taking care of you, you

realize that you haven't had those spinning thoughts that blame your self when you can't figure things out and get settled inside.

Be gentle with your self. You have a lot to think about. You have a lot to learn about who you are, and what you want and don't want for your self.

You have held a double standard for your self.

For her and everyone else, you've given plenty of chances, plenty of room to make mistakes, plenty of understanding and acceptance.

You've been patient and considerate and loving.

By focusing on you and building your self-awareness, you can give your self the same flexibility, the same understanding, and the same acceptance.

You can give your self the same positive acceptance and encouragement you give to everyone else.

You can give your self the same patience, the same consideration, and the same love.

There will be no way to avoid "mistakes"—or what you think are mistakes.

Know that mistakes are really just situations that you would have preferred to have handled in a different way.

You will have to acknowledge and accept that being your self will be an intense journey.

At first, in choosing your self, you will confront feeling different, strange, and guilty. You will probably even feel selfish.

At times, it might feel incredibly disorienting and disturbing.

Yes, you will be afraid, and may end up in your head again with those obsessive, spinning thoughts, feeling disconnected from your self and everyone around you, because nothing feels right to you.

You can learn that those thoughts and fears of being alone for the rest of your life . . . without friends, without a relationship . . . are being magnified by your terrified little kid who has no understanding of time.

With practice, you can learn how to interrupt those moments and comfort your self with a routine, mantra, or action that stops those obsessive little-kid thoughts and brings you back into the present moment.

If you need to, don't be afraid to ask for professional help. Seeking professional help only means that you want the support of someone who can help guide you to understand what is happening for you, and help you find out what you want for your self. We will talk about this suggestion more later on.

In this process, you will learn to feel good about your self, and to value the authentic parts of your self: your needs, your feelings, your thoughts, your preferences, your ideas, your voice, and your power.

You will learn to be your self *out loud*, because you learn to be comfortable being your self.

It won't take long to realize that you're happier when you're learning who you are. The more you learn about your self by connecting your thinking and feelings, the easier it becomes.

And the more confident you become.

Your new relationship perspective, your new emotional perspective, is to be in charge of what you want for your self.

Your touchstone is to value what you think and feel.

CHAPTER 5

THE POSSIBILITY OF SOMETHING MORE—A TWO-PERSON RELATIONSHIP

Feelings just don't change in an instant. Especially feelings of love.

You love her.

As you begin to be your self with her, you will have to accept that your relationship will also change.

In this process you will find out if she wants to be with you when you are trying to be your authentic self, and if there is a possibility of something more.

You must accept that she has the right to her thoughts and feelings.

She too will be deciding whether she wants to be in the relationship when you are changing. She too will be learning whether she wants to change.

The foundation of a two-person relationship is that you are your self and she is her self.

Each of you will have to learn to acknowledge and respect each other's differences.

You will have to accept that she is someone who is separate and different from you.

She will have to accept that you are someone who is separate and different from her.

You will have to accept that she is someone with her own thoughts and feelings, which are different from yours.

She will have to accept that you are someone with your own thoughts and feelings, which are different than hers.

You will have to accept that she is someone whose behaviors, goals, and challenges may bother you, until you come to care about all of her.

She will have to accept that you are someone whose behaviors, goals, and challenges may bother her, until she comes to care about all of you.

You will have to find out if the two of you can build a safe place for the many conversations to come, because you value, trust, and accept each other's unique qualities, thoughts, and feelings, and the resulting viewpoints and behaviors.

Both of you must *want*, more than anything, to learn how to talk together and have discussions. Not little-kid debates or power struggles or physical confrontation.

You will have to find out if you both *want* to build a two-person relationship.

You will know if you're both working to change by paying attention to what you feel when you're together.

You will know if you both are trying to change if you are able to have conversations about her thoughts and preferences *and* your thoughts and preferences.

You will know when you are listening to each other. You'll feel when you both are trying to consider, understand, and value each other's words.

You will know and feel those moments when both of you take responsibility and want to repair the connection between you.

You will be able to feel each other's empathy and caring and efforts to avoid hurting each other. And you'll begin to feel each other's patience and flexibility in your interactions together.

You will feel each other's growing acceptance and understanding.

Or not.

You might have to accept that sometimes a relationship does not work, even though you both feel so much love.

A two-person relationship is about continuing to care and love each other through this difficult process.

It's about learning to help and support each other.

It's about learning to accept and manage each other's needs for intimacy and distance.

It's about learning to talk and listen to each other about the preferences that each of you would like the other to consider.

It's about building a loving "us" connection: you and her.

It's about a connection of integrity, trust, acceptance, caring, and love that you both can feel.

When you value your needs, your feelings, your thoughts, your preferences, your ideas, your voice, and your power, you have something valuable and precious that you bring to a two-person relationship: your self.

BE YOUR SELF

In your life and in your relationships,

Do not take the path

You have always taken.

Instead, blaze a new trail.

It's the one you've never taken.

You will recognize it immediately.

It's the one

You're afraid to take.

ADDENDUM

A NEW RELATIONSHIP PERSPECTIVE

What if You Don't Make It Together

If you leave her because of your emotional pain, you will be devastated.

If she leaves you, you will be devastated.

You will feel lost.

You will be panicked.

You will be inconsolable and depressed.

You will yearn for her in your aloneness.

You will blame your self for having ruined the relationship.

And you will desperately want to reach out to her and do anything that she wants, so she will come back.

But you know she's gone, because you can feel the difference in this leaving.

It's in these painful moments that you can learn how to connect with your self—you and your little kid—and find the idea, the words, the understanding that will help you to remember that if you need her to change and be a different person, then she is not the person you want to be with.

It's very difficult to hold on to and embrace this awareness. It's competing with you and your little kid's giant love for her and the future you thought you could have had together.

So your healing process is about coming to the truth of what happened—accepting your own responsibilities for your part in the demise of the relationship.

And understanding why you tried to do anything and everything for her to try and make her change.

A Place to Start—Seeking Professional Help

There are different paths to becoming one's self and beginning a two-person relationship.

If you're in a one-person relationship then a simple place to start would be to ask her to read our book.

That only requires that she, like you, wants to learn something new about relationship perspectives.

If she is interested in being with you in a new way, it doesn't require talking about each other's needs and feelings. It only requires her interest in learning about you and your relating style and preferences. If and when she's ready to talk about what's happening for her, then that will require your interest in learning about her relating style and preferences.

Learning about each other can start with questions or comments about each other's unique growing-up experiences and challenges.

For those of you who want to talk about your feelings and understand why your relationship is not working, but your partner doesn't want to, individual therapy can help you become self-aware. This can also be helpful if you're no longer in a relationship.

Find a professional who can help you with what's unconscious and automatic about your relating behaviors.

This will help you confirm that your feelings are real,

and that what you feel makes sense. This will help you understand why you keep doing what you do that is so painful.

Most times, you will feel empowered with your new understandings and connections, and it will help you feel better about your self at the end of the session.

Be sure you find someone who will help you interrupt and manage those obsessive spinning thoughts—and can help you understand why you get caught in them.

Be sure you find someone who is caring, nurturing, and understanding—someone who does not cross professional boundaries.

You will feel their caring. You will feel their flexibility. You will feel that they are there for you. You will feel their interest in helping you heal, learn, and grow emotionally.

You will feel their desire to understand you and your perspective—as opposed to having things their way, or assuming they know what's best for you.

Be sure you find someone who does not blame your partner, and who helps you understand the dynamics between you.

Be sure you're also comfortable disagreeing with your therapist, and questioning what doesn't feel right to you.

If they are off-base, or not hearing you, or pushing their feelings on you, or not allowing you the room to be you, then you need to be able to comfortably say what you feel. You need to be able to take care of your self.

If that happens, they should be able to apologize and take responsibility for not understanding you. They should turn their attention back to listening to and wanting to understand your perspective.

If you don't feel like you have the room to say what you want and be heard, then consider finding another therapist.

By being your self, you should experience a two-person relationship with your therapist.

Together, you can come to trust, accept, and value your self. You will learn to talk with the therapist in a clear and unemotional way. You will learn to know what you need and want, and then be able to say it to your partner, directly and calmly, whenever you are ready.

It is then up to your partner to figure out if she is comfortable including you in the relationship.

She might just surprise you, listening to and considering what you are saying, because she doesn't have to deal with your little-kid emotional reactions.

If you both want to seek professional help, it's important to know that different therapies and therapists will resonate with you and your partner. Look into a therapy process that feels right for you both as individuals—one in which each of you can safely express your own thoughts and feelings.

Sometimes, however, it is very difficult for couples to remain calm enough in therapy to learn new ways of listening and talking together.

There are also couples who can't go into therapy together because one or both partners can't or won't talk about their feelings.

If this is your situation, you might explore Imago Relationship Therapy. It was developed by Harville Hendrix, PhD, and Helen LaKelly Hunt, PhD. It utilizes a structured format called the Imago Dialogue. You can find a therapist to facilitate your dialogue, or join a workshop, learning to build a place of emotional safety for listening and talking together, without your emotions getting in the way.

The goal of the Imago Dialogue is to begin to experience and accept each other's differences and "otherness." At the same time, it is designed to encourage, guide, and support the two of you as you learn to work together.

You can quickly begin to experience the concept of two-person relating in this therapy process.

Look for therapists who are certified in Imago Therapy.

If the cost of therapy is a concern, ask your therapist if they work on a sliding scale. If not, inquire about group therapy.

You can also call or visit your religious center, and ask for their recommendations.

Or you can check with your city community centers, to see if they offer free or low-cost counseling.

There are also low-cost clinics which will bill on a sliding scale.

You can also call local colleges and universities to see if they train and supervise mental health professionals, offering a reduced rate through an affiliated counseling center.

Counseling services are also available online.

Couples who don't want to go into therapy have a different challenge, as their emotional work will be driven by their individual commitments to become themselves and find out if their relationship can begin to work, without a moderator or facilitator.

Through trial and error and a lot of patience, couples can try to talk together, on their own, while learning to manage and eliminate their little-kid responses.

As you begin to talk about and acknowledge each other's differences in whatever venue you choose, your two-person commitment is tested every step of the way.

Each step—each decision in discovering how best to talk about your preferences and your differences—is a two-person relationship decision, because now you have included your self in determining what happens. If one of you doesn't agree, then another solution must be found together, or one of you will confront having to give up your self for the other, or make a decision to leave.

Moving towards a two-person relationship takes commitment and hard emotional work on the part of both individuals.

Your relationship becomes a two-person relationship as each of you learns to focus on your own needs and feelings, expressing your own preferences, at the same time that you learn to consider each other's feelings and preferences.

This happens when you want to support each other's emotional potential and growth and independence. And inspire . . . one another.

And it happens when you respect and value each other's need to be them selves.

Additional Thoughts to Consider

1. There is a difference in your relationship perspectives. She can feel one way and you can feel another, and both your feelings and her feelings can be true in the same moment. Neither one of you is right or wrong. You are simply feeling and interpreting things differently as separate individuals.

2. Understand there's a reason she needs to be in charge.

   As a child, she, too, had an important parent like you did, and she *won't* give up herself now.

   Consider another possibility: she got everything she ever wanted as a child, and now she expects to get everything she wants from you.

   Consider, too, that there's another reason, which only she can share.

3. Through your conversations with her, you may come to the realization that even though you believed that she was in charge, she feels that she was in charge because she thought that's what you wanted.

4. It's best if you make a choice to change for your self, instead of waiting for her to make the decision for you. That way you'll be more committed to and more accepting of the challenges that go along with choosing your self.

If she left you or if you left her because of your emotional pain, you're going to feel rejected and hurt. The thoughts in your head will not be about taking care of your self, you'll be trying to keep a lid on figuring out why she left you or you left her and what you could have done differently.

5. If being your self doesn't appeal to you, or if it sounds like too much work, you could decide to leave and look for someone new. Someone who will be happy to change herself to take care of your emotional needs, because she loves you so much.

    Know you'd be looking for someone just like you. Someone who will give up themselves.

Visit us and view more at
http://maureenehosierphd.com.

Please share your stories and join my blog on my website, as you begin to understand your giving style of relating. Let us know what you are thinking and feeling as you learn about your self and start your journey to a two-person relationship.

ABOUT THE AUTHORS

MAUREEN E. HOSIER

Maureen has worked as a licensed psychologist in California since 1993. Her career focus has been the study of the psychological forces that underlie the behaviors, feelings, and emotions between people in relationships. She has specifically been interested in how a child's lack of development of self-esteem and self-confidence within a parent-child relationship, influences their adult style, patterns, and cycles of relating.

BERTA HOSIER CONGER

Berta has a Bachelor of Science degree in psychology from Ohio State University. But she pursued a different career path, because at the time of her graduation, only PhD candidates were being hired. She went on to build a thirty-year career in banking and investments. Her desire to help her sister co-author a book on relationships was driven by her need to integrate the two people she sensed inside her. She felt that she was her self at work, but she wasn't her self in her relationships. She knew she had two distinct, parallel lives, but had no idea why it was happening, or how to integrate the two.

ABOUT MAUREEN AND BERTA

Maureen always wanted to write a book about relationships, but knew she couldn't do it on her own. She couldn't get it down on paper without her sister's focus on detail, organization, and flow—not to mention her sister's ability to bring introspective depth and richness to their combined understanding of one-person and two-person relationships.

Writing the book together became their way of learning how to be in a two-person relationship.

Toward this goal, it took some time for them to find their way to a two-person emotional language. Through their conversations and written exchanges, they learned to listen to each other.

It took a lot of talking and getting *in it!* for the sisters as they worked together on this book. Then more talking, yelling, and shutting down. Then more talking. Then more listening, patience, and flexibility.

Eventually they learned how to not ruin the moments between them.

It also took persistence and acceptance to figure out how to push toward the finish line without each needing to control the other.

Even as the book is almost finished, the sisters are still learning how to use their little-kid moments to help them understand about one-person relating, and why it's so difficult to build a two-person relationship, given their beginnings in a one-person household.

They learned that nothing could be accomplished unless they learned to value, accept, and explore each other's new ideas and suggested rewrites, and accept how and when the ideas and rewrites came about.

They learned that the book would be complete when it was "right" for them both.

Learning to be in a two-person relationship takes time. It takes commitment. It takes a lot of hard emotional work.

The sisters are still learning how to accept each other as persons who are separate from what each wants the other to be.

They are still learning to trust the process between them and to appreciate each other's contribution and differences.

And they are still learning how to take care of their own selves and respectively communicate their preferences.

ACKNOWLEDGMENTS

We would like to thank our parents and send them our love and understanding for raising us in the only way they knew how—for it has brought us and our readers the opportunity to learn about one-person relationships. We now understand that this was as difficult and painful for them as it was for us. We now know that they wanted to give us the best foundation for living a life that demanded strength, determination, persistence, and fortitude.

They cared for us, they cared about us, and they did the best they could do for us, based on their own experiences and teachings from their parents.

Just like them, we didn't know what we didn't know, until we learned a new relationship perspective.

We would also like to acknowledge and thank our parents for teaching us the power of never giving up and standing up for what we believe. Our persistence is, and has been, the key that keeps us learning how to be equal and respectful in our relationships as we learn to be comfortable being our selves, and as we learn how to be in a two-person relationship with each other, our partners, and our family and friends.

We would also like to give special recognition to those people who have helped us on our journey to this book. Your interest, support, encouragement, and involvement in our vision was critical to our staying on track, because you too felt that our words were true for you and would benefit others.

You know who you are. Thank you for your valuable, wise, and heartfelt contributions.

A SPECIAL ACKNOWLEDGMENT TO MY CLIENTS

I would especially like to thank my clients for trusting me with the deepest parts of themselves as we journey together to find and value their selves.

Maureen E. Hosier PhD

RESOURCES

DISCLAIMER

The authors are providing the resources listed below as a convenience to our readers.

The authors are not responsible for the reader's choices in finding a licensed professional to help them with their unique and specific issues and concerns, nor should these resources be considered recommendations by the coauthors.

1. *Psychology Today.*
   https://therapists.psychologytoday.com/rms/

   You can search for therapists first by zip code, then by issues. For example: relationship issues, self-esteem, family conflict, codependence, domestic violence, etc. You can also search by other parameters such as support groups, insurance, treatment orientation, age, faith, etc.

2. *The American Association of Family Therapy and Educational Foundation.*
   http://www.therapistlocator.net/

   The therapists on this site are listed first by zip code, then individually by last name, with a link to a description of their specialty.

3. Imago Therapy is a style of relationship therapy that utilizes a specific format, called the Imago Dialogue, to develop listening and communication skills. The Imago Dialogue promotes the building of understanding and empathy between the partners.
   http://www.imagorelationships.org/

4. Codependents Anonymous (CODA). "A 12-step fellowship of men and women whose purpose is to develop healthy relationships."
   http://coda.org/

FURTHER READINGS

Some of these works are available in multiple editions—our advice is to read the edition that is easiest to obtain.

Beattie, Melody. *Codependent No More: How to Stop Controlling Others and Start Caring for Yourself.*

Beattie, Melody. *The Language of Letting Go: Daily Meditations for Codependents.*

Beattie, Melody. *The New Codependency: Help and Guidance for Today's Generation.*

Chapman, Gary. *The 5 Love Languages: The Secret to Love That Lasts.*

Chapman, Gary. *Everybody Wins. The Chapman Guide to Solving Conflicts without Arguing.*

Davis, Martha, PhD; Elizabeth Robbins Eshelman, MSW; and Matthew McKay, PhD. *The Relaxation and Stress Reduction Workbook.*

Dennis, Sandra Lee. *Love and the Mystery of Betrayal: Recovering Your Trust and Faith after Trauma, Deception, and Loss of Love.*

Elliot, Susan J. *Getting Past Your Breakup: How to Turn a Devastating Loss into the Best Thing that Ever Happened to You.*

Gibson, Lindsay C., PsyD. *Adult Children of Emotionally Immature Parents: How to Heal from Distant, Rejecting, or Self-Involved Parents.*

Hendrix, Harville, PhD. *Getting the Love You Need. A Guide for Couples.* Twentieth Anniversary Edition.

Hendrix, Harville, PhD. *Keeping the Love You Find: A Personal Guide.*

Hendrix, Harville, PhD, and Helen Hunt, MA, MLA. *Giving the Love that Heals: A Guide for Parents.*

Hornor Plumez, Jacqueline, PhD. *The Bitch in Your Head: How to Finally Squash Your Inner Critic.*

Kaplan, Louise J., PhD. *Oneness and Separateness: From Infant to Individual.*

Keyes, Ken, Jr. *A Conscious Person's Guide to Relationships.*

Johnson, Spencer. *Who Moved My Cheese? An Amazing Way to Deal with Change in Your Work and Life.* Rep. Ed.

Levine, Amir, M.D. and Rachel S.F. Heller, M.A. *Attached: New Science of Adult Attachment and How It Can Help You Find—and Keep—Love.*

Nakazawa, Donna. *Childhood Disrupted: How Your Biography Becomes Your Biology, and How You Can Heal.*

Norwood, Robin. *Women Who Love Too Much: When You Keep Wishing and Hoping He Will Change.*

Paul, Jordan, and Margaret Paul, PhD. *Do I Have to Give Up Me to Be Loved by You?*

CPSIA information can be obtained
at www.ICGtesting.com
Printed in the USA
LVOW01s1345190417
531388LV00016B/304/P